Edgar Degas

BY LINDA CERNAK • ILLUSTRATED BY J. T. MORROW

Published by The Child's World®
1980 Lookout Drive • Mankato, MN 56003-1705
800-599-READ • www.childsworld.com

Acknowledgments
The Child's World®: Mary Berendes, Publishing Director
Red Line Editorial: Editorial direction and production
The Design Lab: Design

Photographs ©: Edgar Degas, cover, 1, 6, 9, 12, 13, 15,
17; Alfredo Dagli Orti/The Art Archive/Corbis, 5; Giancarlo
Liguori/Shutterstock Images, 8; Corbis, 10; Bettmann/Corbis,
19; Stoyan Nenov/Reuters/Corbis, 21

ISBN 9781626873490
LCCN 2014930688

Printed in the United States of America
Mankato, MN
July, 2014
PA02223

ABOUT THE AUTHOR

Linda Cernak has more than 35 years of experience as a freelance writer and in-house editor of children's classroom readers and student textbooks. Since 1994, Cernak has published numerous children's books in the subject areas of social studies, science, and the arts. In her spare time, Cernak enjoys painting, drawing, and creating stained glass sculptures.

ABOUT THE ILLUSTRATOR

J.T. Morrow has worked as a freelance illustrator for more than 25 years and has won several awards. His work has appeared in advertisements, on packaging, in magazines, and in books. He lives near San Francisco, California, with his wife and daughter.

CONTENTS

CHAPTER 1

A New Kind of Art

THE IMPRESSIONISTS

The Impressionists got their name from an oil painting done by the artist Claude Monet. Monet had painted a picture of a sunrise. He called it Impression, Sunrise. *He used very loose brushstrokes. It didn't have precise, clean lines. The painting shocked the art world. But it paved the way for a new style of art.*

The year was 1865. The city of Paris, France, was alive with activity. It was the center of the Western art world. In the late 1800s, artists were trying different ways of painting. They broke rules Western artists had followed for a long time. They experimented with colors and light. They began to paint outdoors. Artists had never painted like this before. These artists would become known as the **Impressionists**. One of these artists was Edgar Degas.

At first Degas painted pictures similar to those of many artists before him. These artists were called the **classical** artists. They had followed strict rules. Their paintings showed people who were posed. Classical artists painted events that happened long ago.

Edgar Degas painted this portrait of himself in 1863.

But then Degas began to paint the world around him. He painted people doing everyday things. He painted dancers and singers. His paintings swirled with brilliant colors. Degas wanted to capture a moment in time. He did not like to paint posed figures. Many of his paintings looked like **candid** shots.

Degas's Portrait in a New Orleans Cotton Office *shows businessmen experiencing their everyday lives.*

Degas and other Impressionists shocked the people of Paris. Their paintings did not follow the rules. Their style of painting was very different from classical paintings. Sometimes objects in the paintings weren't very clear. But people began to notice Degas's work. They liked his scenes of life in Paris. Degas's paintings became very popular in Paris.

CHAPTER 2
An Art Show of Their Own

Edgar Degas was born in Paris in 1834. His father knew Edgar had a talent for painting. So he often took Edgar to the Louvre. This is a famous museum in Paris. Edgar loved to copy the classical paintings he saw. He began to study art at the best art schools in Paris.

During the 1860s, artists wanted to show their works at an important art show in Paris. It was called the Salon.

Today, the Louvre in Paris is still home to many famous paintings.

This show was held every year. At the Salon, huge rooms were filled with paintings. Judges reviewed the paintings. They favored paintings that followed the strict rules of classical art. Artists could become great successes if the judges liked their paintings.

Degas showed some of his paintings at the Salon in 1865. His paintings showed scenes from history. He also painted classical **portraits**. The judges loved his paintings. But Degas did not want to paint classical paintings. Instead, he wanted to paint scenes of everyday life. It was a new idea in the art world. It was an idea that would make Degas famous.

Degas showed his historical painting Scene of War in the Middle Ages *at the Salon in 1865.*

Degas's family was very wealthy. So he did not have to worry about selling his paintings for money. But in 1874, Degas's father died. His father had owed people a lot of money. This meant Degas would need to begin selling his paintings. Judges at the Salon did not like Impressionist paintings. So Degas formed a group with other Impressionist artists. The artists decided to have their own show instead.

Degas showed ten of his paintings at the show. His works showed scenes from everyday life. Dancers, horses and racers, and women doing laundry covered his canvases. People liked Degas's paintings.

At the show, people did not like most of the other Impressionist paintings. They were confused by the style of the paintings. The colors were too bold. Some paintings,

Degas showed At the Races in the Countryside *at the 1874 art show.*

such as Claude Monet's *Impression, Sunrise*, looked blurry. Other paintings did not look finished. People were not used to the way the Impressionists painted.

Artists before this usually painted in **studios**. But many of the Impressionists took their easels outdoors to paint **landscapes**. They painted by using light, quick brushstrokes. They liked to show how the light on objects changed as the sun moved across the sky.

Degas's paintings were a little different from those of the other Impressionist artists. In fact, Degas did not want to be called an Impressionist at all. He did not like to paint outdoors. He liked to make a lot of **sketches**. Then he would use the sketches to paint in his studio.

Degas especially liked to paint dancers. He would go backstage, where dancers were practicing. There, he would make sketches. He liked to study and sketch the way the human body moved. And he loved the dancers' pretty costumes. Then he took the sketches to his studio. There, he carefully painted the dancers in different poses. Degas became well known in Paris for these lovely paintings.

Degas showed different points of view in his paintings. He liked to show a different **perspective**. Sometimes he would only show part of a dancer. Or he would sometimes paint as if he were looking down at the dancers.

Degas liked to sketch many of his subjects, such as this dancer, before painting them.

In many of his works, it feels as if you are part of the painting.

The Rehearsal is one of Degas's many paintings of dancers.

CHAPTER 3

Painting and Drawing Everyday Life

Degas loved to paint pictures of everyday scenes. He painted hundreds of pictures of horse races. The jockeys in his paintings wore bright costumes. The paintings captured the excitement of the horse race.

Many of Degas's paintings showed people doing ordinary things. Some showed women shopping for hats. Others were of women doing laundry. Degas painted pictures of women doing very personal things, too. A painting might show a woman after a bath or a woman combing her hair.

At first these paintings were shocking. People were not used to seeing these scenes in artwork. But Degas wanted to show the lives of normal people. Some people may have thought this was strange. Instead, Degas thought of himself as a painter of modern life. His works were beautifully painted with rich colors. People began buying Degas's works.

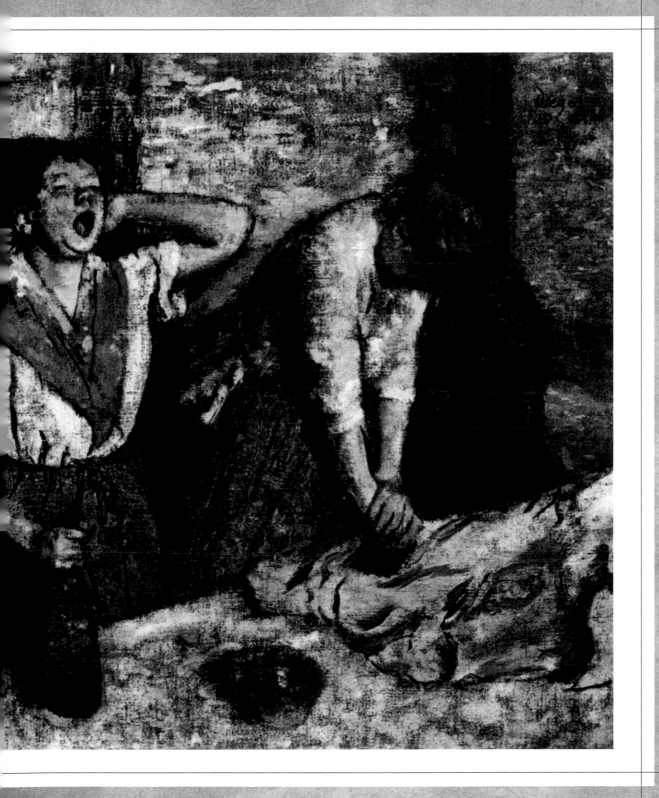

Degas watched women as they worked and depicted their
everyday actions, as in Laundry Girls Ironing.

Singers were another one of Degas's favorite subjects. There were many theater cafés in Paris. They were alive with singers. Degas loved the way the light fell upon the singers on stage. Their bright, colorful costumes lit up under the lights. Degas had used oil colors to paint many of his works. But he began to use **pastels** in his paintings of singers and dancers.

Degas drew hundreds of pictures with pastels. He drew the same subjects over and over. The pastel colors were dazzling and bright. Jockeys and horses streaked across a painting as if they were moving. Dancers yawned and stretched. And singers glowed with color. The colors made the drawings come alive with movement.

PASTELS

Pastels are like colored crayons. They are made from colored powders and gum. Oil paints take a long time to dry. Pastels do not have to dry. This is why Degas could create so many pastel drawings so quickly. With pastels, an artist can make interesting and bright strokes. Pastels can also make a soft shade of color.

Why do their dresses look fuzzy?

Degas used pastels to draw Four Dancers on Stage.

CHAPTER 4

Photographs and Sculptures

By the time Degas was in his 60s, he was a very famous artist. People came from all over to buy his paintings. In the early 1890s, Degas discovered photography. He bought a box camera. Soon he began taking pictures of the countryside. He took pictures of his friends and family, too.

Today, only about 50 of Degas's photographs exist. Like his paintings, the photographs are works of art. Degas studied his photos when he painted pictures. He would cut, or **crop**, part of the photo. Then he would paint a picture of the cropped part. The photos were cropped to make interesting angles. Part of a person in a painting might be cut off. The paintings looked just like a real photo a person might take.

PHOTOGRAPHY

Photography is the art of taking pictures with a camera. The first real camera was invented in the 1830s. These early cameras were big and bulky. Then, in 1888, Kodak came out with a camera you could hold in your hands. It was a handheld box camera.

As Degas grew older, he began to lose his eyesight. It was hard for him to paint.

He could not see what he painted very well. So he started creating new art: **sculptures**. Instead of painting dancers, he sculpted them from wax.

Degas's most famous sculpture is a bronze statue of a dancer. He dressed the dancer in a real tutu and slippers. He even put a ribbon in her hair. People were shocked. They had never seen a statue dressed in real clothes before!

Degas continued to make wax sculptures. But he could no longer see well enough to paint. Young artists admired his works. They wanted to talk with him and learn from him. Degas enjoyed being famous. But as he grew older and lost his eyesight, he wanted to be left alone. Degas died in 1917. When his family came to his house, they were surprised at what they found. Degas left hundreds of beautiful paintings behind. Dozens of wax figures danced around his apartment. People came from all over to buy the works of the famous artist.

Degas was a different kind of Impressionist. He found a way to place everyday life into his oil paintings, pastel drawings, and sculptures. Sketches and photography helped him create his beautiful works of art. He is still known today for his unique style. Degas truly captured the beauty of his time in his art.

What do you think of Degas's statue?

Degas's Little Dancer of Fourteen Years *sculpture still surprises viewers with its real cloth skirt and hair ribbon.*

Glossary

candid (KAN-did) To take a candid shot in photography is to take a picture of subjects that are not posed. Degas liked to paint candid pictures of dancers.

classical (KLAS-i-kuhl) Classical art follows a traditional or older style. Impressionist art was very new and different from classical art.

crop (KRAHP) To crop is to cut off the ends or edges of something. Degas liked to crop the photographs he took.

Impressionists (im-PRESH-uhn-ists) Impressionists were French painters of the late 1800s who formed a new style of art. Degas was an Impressionist artist. He liked to experiment with color, light, and perspective.

landscapes (LAND-skapes) Landscapes are large areas of land that can be seen in one view. Many Impressionist artists liked to go outdoors to paint landscapes.

pastels (pa-STELS) Pastels are crayons that are similar to chalk. Degas sketched many of his works using pastels.

perspective (pur-SPEK-tiv) Painting in perspective is giving a flat image an appearance of distance and depth. Degas used perspective in his paintings to make dancers appear either closer or farther away.

portraits (POR-trits) Portraits are pictures of a person's face. Degas's classical portraits were well liked by judges at the Salon.

sculptures (SKUHLP-churs) Sculptures are carved and shaped out of stone, clay, wood, or other materials. Degas began creating sculptures later in his life.

sketches (SKECH-ez) Sketches are rough or beginning drawings. Degas often drew sketches of his subjects, such as dancers, before painting or drawing them.

studios (STOO-dee-ohz) Studios are rooms or buildings in which an artist works. While many Impressionists left their studios to paint outdoors, Degas preferred to paint in his studio.

To Learn More

BOOKS

Mis, Melody S. *Edgar Degas*. New York: PowerKids Press, 2008.

Spence, David. *The Great Artists and Their World: Degas.* Mankato, MN: Newforest Press, 2010.

WEB SITES

Visit our Web site for links about Edgar Degas:

childsworld.com/links

Note to Parents, Teachers, and Librarians:
We routinely verify our Web links to make sure they are safe and active sites. So encourage your readers to check them out!

Index